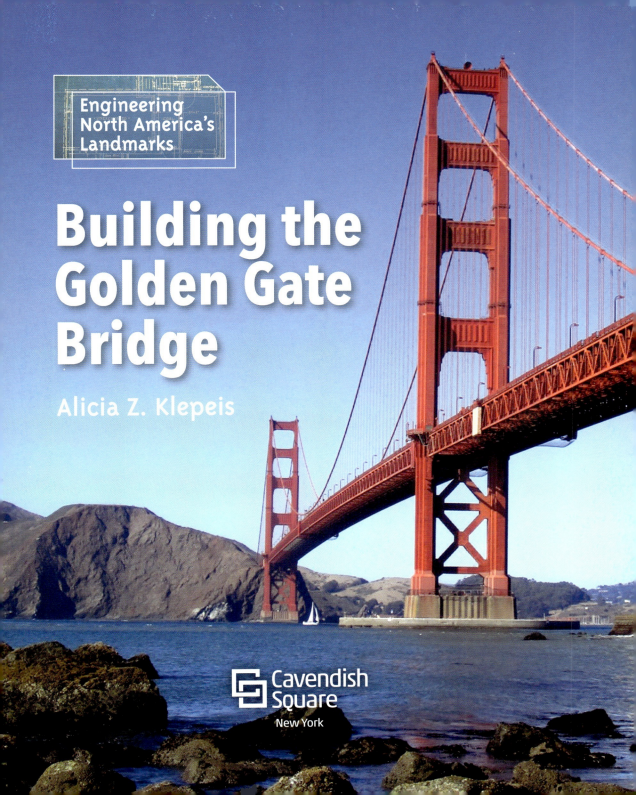

Published in 2018 by Cavendish Square Publishing, LLC
243 5th Avenue, Suite 136, New York, NY 10016

Copyright © 2018 by Cavendish Square Publishing, LLC

First Edition

No part of this publication may be reproduced, stored in a retrieval system, or transmitted in any form or by any means—electronic, mechanical, photocopying, recording, or otherwise—without the prior permission of the copyright owner. Request for permission should be addressed to Permissions, Cavendish Square Publishing, 243 5th Avenue, Suite 136, New York, NY 10016. Tel (877) 980-4450; fax (877) 980-4454.

Website: cavendishsq.com

This publication represents the opinions and views of the author based on his or her personal experience, knowledge, and research. The information in this book serves as a general guide only. The author and publisher have used their best efforts in preparing this book and disclaim liability rising directly or indirectly from the use and application of this book.

All websites were available and accurate when this book was sent to press.

Library of Congress Cataloging-in-Publication Data

Names: Klepeis, Alicia, 1971- author.
Title: Building the Golden Gate Bridge / Alicia Z. Klepeis.
Description: New York : Cavendish Square Publishing, [2018] | Series: Engineering North America's landmarks | Includes bibliographical references index.
Identifiers: LCCN 2017015900 (print) | LCCN 2017022837 (ebook) | ISBN 9781502629678 (E-book) | ISBN 9781502629647 (pbk.) | ISBN 9781502629661 (library bound) | ISBN 9781502629654 (6 pack)
Subjects: LCSH: Golden Gate Bridge (San Francisco, Calif.)--Juvenile literature. | Suspension bridges--California--San Francisco--Design and construction--History--Juvenile literature. | San Francisco (Calif.)--Buildings, structures, etc.--Juvenile literature.
Classification: LCC TG25.S225 (ebook) | LCC TG25.S225 K54 2018 (print) | DDC 624.2/30979461--dc23
LC record available at https://lccn.loc.gov/2017015900

Editorial Director: David McNamara
Editor: Fletcher Doyle
Copy Editor: Rebecca Rohan
Associate Art Director: Amy Greenan
Designer: Alan Sliwinski
Production Coordinator: Karol Szymczuk
Photo Research: J8 Media

The photographs in this book are used by permission and through the courtesy of: Francis1203/Wikimedia Commons/File:Golden Gate Bridge taken from Baker Beach.JPG/CC BY SA 3.0; p. 4 Enrique R. Aguirre Aves/Alamy Stock Photo; p. 6 Universal History Archive/UIG/Getty Images; p. 7 USGS/Wikimedia Commons/File:BayareaUSGS.jpg/Public Domain; p. 8 Everett Historical/Shutterstock.com; p. 9, 22, 23 Bettmann/Getty Images; p. 11 Pavalena/Shutterstock.com; p. 12 Michael Howell/ Perspectives/Getty Images; p. 15 Matthias079/Wikimedia Commons/File:Suspension bridge pattern german1.svg/CC BY SA 2.5; p. 16, 17 Underwood Archives/Getty Images; p 19 Bettmann/Getty Images; p. 20 Francesco Carucci/Shutterstock.com; p. 24 San Francisco History Center, San Francisco Public Library; p. 26 Red monkey/Shutterstock.com.

Printed in the United States of America

Contents

Chapter One	A Golden Idea	5
	Golden Gate Bridge by the Numbers	10
Chapter Two	Construction and Problems	13
Chapter Three	A Bridge for the Ages	21
	Golden Gate Bridge Quiz	28
	Glossary	29
	Find Out More	30
	Index	31
	About the Author	32

Ferries were once the only way across the Golden Gate Strait.

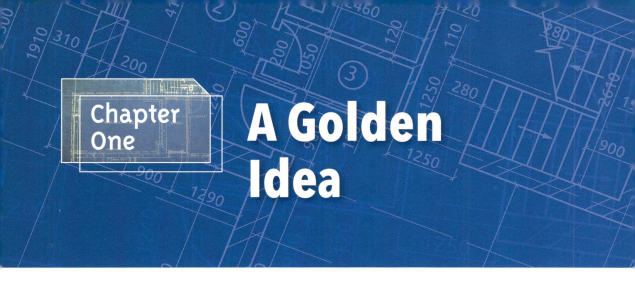

Chapter One: A Golden Idea

You're cruising into San Francisco Bay on a ferryboat. As you're standing on the deck, the fog is thick. Seagulls call overhead. Minutes later, the fog lifts. In front of you stands the bright orange Golden Gate Bridge.

Today, this bridge is a famous landmark. Years ago, people thought it could not be built. Why? Deep water. Strong **currents**. Earthquakes. Cost.

It took dreamers to create the Golden Gate Bridge. It took people who could see the future.

A Booming City

In the 1840s, San Francisco was a small town. Before the **Gold Rush**, only a few hundred people lived there. By 1849, the population had boomed to thirty-five thousand.

This illustration shows San Francisco and its bay in the 1850s. The city's population was starting to boom.

People needed to travel between San Francisco and Marin County. There was only one way to cross San Francisco Bay. That was by ferry. The wait for the ferry to come could take hours. Something had to be done.

This satellite photo shows the San Francisco Bay area. The Golden Gate Strait runs between the Pacific Ocean and San Francisco Bay.

Bridge Dreams

Charles Crocker became president of the Southern Pacific Railroad in 1871.

The ferry crossed the Golden Gate Strait. A strait is a narrow passage connecting two large bodies of water. Charles Crocker was the president of the Southern Pacific Railroad. In 1872, Crocker said that engineers had plans to put a railroad bridge across the strait. This bridge would carry railroad cars. Experts thought Crocker's idea wouldn't work. Nothing happened with his idea.

Fast forward to 1919. Michael O'Shaughnessy was San Francisco's City Engineer. City officials asked him to do a study. They wondered if a bridge could be built across the strait. O'Shaughnessy met with engineers. He talked to scientists. He met with bridge builders. A bridge builder named Joseph Strauss said a bridge could be built there. He sketched designs for this bridge.

Engineers C.E. Payne (*left*) and Joseph B. Strauss (*right*) inspect the bridge.

Fast Fact
The first Golden Gate Bridge design was turned down. Critics said it was ugly. One called it "an upside-down rat trap."

Golden Gate Bridge by the Numbers

Time of Construction: From January 5, 1933 to April 27, 1937

Construction Cost: $35 million ($630 million in today's money)

Total Length of Bridge: 1.7 miles (2.7 kilometers)

Length of Span Between Towers: 1.2 miles (1.9 km)

Clearance Above Water: 220 feet (67 meters) at high tide

Weird Fact: A lot of concrete was used for the bridge. There was enough to make a 5-foot-wide (1.5 m) sidewalk from San Francisco to New York.

Building the Golden Gate Bridge

Time to approve the project: It took fourteen years. A design was proposed in 1916. The final permit was given August 11, 1930.

Cable Connection: The two main cables contain 80,000 miles (128,750 km) of wire. That's enough to circle the globe more than three times.

San Francisco's Golden Gate Bridge is located in Northern California.

A Golden Idea

The Golden Gate Bridge is arched, so it won't sag with a heavy load.

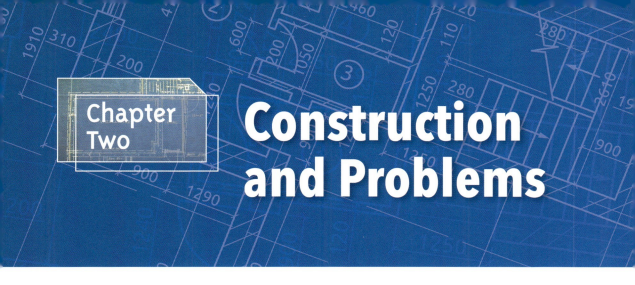

Chapter Two
Construction and Problems

The Golden Gate project tested bridge designers. Joseph Strauss's team had to think about forces that could affect the bridge. **Compression** and **tension** are key forces. Compression pushes things together. Tension pulls them apart.

What causes these forces? Loads.

All bridges support two kinds of loads. One is the weight of the structure. This is the "dead" load. The other is the weight of anything crossing the bridge. Examples are cars or people. This is the "live" load. The bridge had to hold both loads.

Other forces are natural. The bridge had to resist strong winds. It had to survive earthquakes. The San Andreas **Fault** is just 5.6 miles (9 km) away. The bridge had to stand up against strong currents. It had to support many vehicles. It had to be built on solid bedrock. The bedrock supports the bridge's towers.

Four Parts

The Golden Gate Bridge is a suspension bridge. There are four main parts of a suspension bridge: **anchorages**, towers, cables, and decking.

Workers built the anchorages first. Anchorages are huge blocks of concrete. These blocks grip the

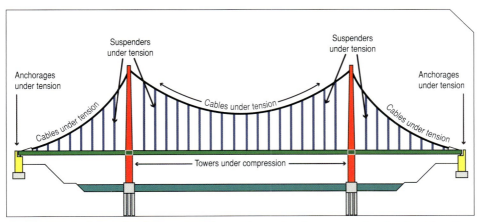

This diagram shows the forces at work on the parts of a suspension bridge. Tension is caused by stretching. Compression is caused by being pressed together.

cables that hold up the bridge. They are needed at both ends of the Golden Gate Strait. They are made of steel frames filled with concrete.

After the anchorages came two piers. Piers were needed to support the towers. They had to rest on solid bedrock. The piers had to be level.

Next came the bridge's towers. They stand 746 feet (227 meters) above the water's surface.

Cables and Building the Road

The Golden Gate Bridge has two giant main cables. These cables rest on saddles on top of each tower. The cables receive the tension forces of the bridge. These forces travel along the cables and pass into the anchorages. Other cables hang from the

Workers bundle many thin wires so they can be made into one thick cable.

The bridge's roadbed was suspended from hanging cables in 1936. The roadbed was made of steel frames.

two main ones. They support the road. They are called suspenders. The loads put tension on the suspenders.

Spinning the Cables

The cables supporting the Golden Gate Bridge are not solid. They are made of thin wire. Yet these cables can support 400 million pounds (181,437 metric tons). How can such thin wire be so strong? When spun with other wires, it gets stronger.

The finished cables would have been too heavy to lift into place. They had to be made on site.

> **Fast Fact**
> The bridge's road can move up and down. It can go side to side. This lets the road adjust to a changing load. A stiff road could break apart in storms or earthquakes.

Workers spun 80,000 miles (128,747 km) of thin wire into strands. A wheel spun the wire across the strait and back. Machines **compacted** these strands into bundles. More than twenty-seven thousand steel wires made up each cable. Each cable is 7,650 feet (2,332 meters) long. They were wrapped in wire **sheaths** for protection.

John Roebling invented a way to spin steel cables. His company found a way to spin six wires at one time. This made cable making faster.

Strauss's team attached the steel frame for the road. The frame hung from the suspenders. They poured concrete into the frame for the roadbed.

Bridge Builder

John Roebling's wire spinner.

John Roebling was an engineer. He was born in Germany in 1806. He wanted to build suspension bridges. No one in Germany would let him. So he moved to the United States.

Roebling invented wire ropes that were much stronger than hemp ropes. He used them to build the first railroad suspension bridge. It crossed the Niagara River into Canada. Roebling died after an accident in 1869. He was working on the Brooklyn Bridge. His son finished that bridge. His sons built up his company. It spun the Golden Gate Bridge's cables.

The thick fog can make it hard to see the Golden Gate Bridge.

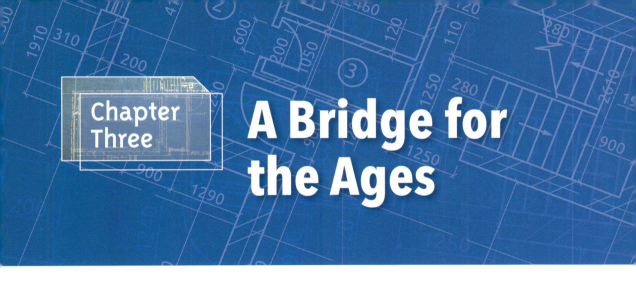

Chapter Three
A Bridge for the Ages

Joseph Strauss's team created a bridge no one would forget. No one had ever built a suspension bridge with such a long span. The span is the space between the towers. It took more than four years to finish. People first walked across it on May 27, 1937.

Every worker played a role. Some poured concrete. Others hammered **rivets** or painted the steel. Its bright orange color helps ship captains see it in the fog.

Pier Problems

There were problems building the south pier for the Golden Gate Bridge.

Workers ran into problems. One was with the bedrock where the south pier was planned. It was too soft. The pier was built more than 1,100 feet (335 m) from shore. The water there was rough and deep. It was often inky black. That made it hard for divers building the pier to see.

A supported road led out to the pier site. On August 14, 1933, the fog was thick. Crash! A freighter smashed into a **trestle**. The trestle supporting the road was fixed. Then a storm hit it in autumn 1933. It had to be rebuilt. The south pier was finished in January 1935.

Safety Comes First

Construction sites in the 1930s weren't as safe as they are today. People thought that for every one million dollars of construction costs, one person would be killed. Joseph Strauss felt that was too high a price. During this project, safety procedures were introduced. For example, workers had to wear safety helmets.

The Golden Gate project's most famous safety measure was a net. Putting up the steel for the roadway was very dangerous. Strauss had

A huge safety net saved the lives of many bridge workers.

a giant net made. It cost more than $130,000. It hung below the roadway. If a workman slipped, he'd fall into the net. Nineteen workers were saved by the net.

A Terrible Day

Strauss's safety measures helped many workers. For more than three years, no workers died. One man was killed by a falling beam on October 21, 1936. Then on the morning of February 17, 1937, tragedy struck.

Crowds inspect a plaque for workers who died building the bridge. This photo was taken May 27, 1937.

> **Fast Fact**
> More than two billion vehicles have crossed the Golden Gate Bridge since it opened on May 28, 1937.

A five-ton (4,536 kg) platform at the north tower broke loose. It ripped through the safety net. Twelve men fell hundreds of feet into the water. Nine died right away. Another died of injuries later. Two men survived the fall. Eleven men died in all.

What caused the platform failure? Its bolts were too short to hold it.

Legacy of the Golden Gate Bridge

Today, the Golden Gate Bridge is one of America's most famous landmarks. The technology developed helped in the construction of other bridges. Strauss's safety measures are still used.

The Golden Gate Bridge has become a symbol for San Francisco and all of the Bay Area.

This bridge makes traveling easier for Bay Area residents. It helps tourists, also. More than ten million people visit the bridge each year!

The Golden Gate Bridge inspires artists and writers. Even Joseph Strauss wrote a poem about it. The poem reads in part:

At last the mighty task is done;
Resplendent in the western sun
The Bridge looms mountain high;
Its titan piers grip ocean floor,
Its great steel arms link shore with shore,
Its towers pierce the sky.

Longest US Suspension Bridge Spans

1. Verrazano-Narrows Bridge The New York City bridge has a span 4,260 feet (1,298 m) long.

2. Golden Gate Bridge Its span of 4,200 feet (1,280 m) was the world's longest until 1964.

3. Mackinac Bridge The more than 5-mile (8 km) bridge across the Mackinac Straits has a longest span of 3,800 feet (1,158 m).

4. George Washington Bridge This landmark across the Hudson River has a span of 3,500 feet (1,067 m).

5. Tacoma Narrows Bridge This bridge across Puget Sound has a span of 2,800 feet (853 m).

Golden Gate Bridge Quiz

1. How long did it take to build the Golden Gate Bridge?

2. In what state is the Golden Gate Bridge located?

3. Which river did the first railroad suspension bridge cross?

4. Were any workers killed during the bridge's construction?

Answers
1. A little more than four years
2. California
3. The Niagara River.
4. Yes. Eleven men died while the bridge was being built.

Glossary

anchorage Concrete structures that hold suspension cables at each end of a bridge.

compact To put force on something to make it more dense (or packed together).

compression The act or force that presses things together.

current Fast-moving water flowing in one direction.

fault A break in the earth's crust where plates collide or pull apart. This is where earthquakes start.

Gold Rush The period from 1848 to 1855 when many people moved to California seeking gold.

rivet A short metal bolt or pin used to hold two plates of metal together.

sheath A close-fitting covering for something, such as a cable.

tension The force where something is being stretched to the point of stiffness.

trestle A braced frame that supports a bridge.

Find Out More

Books

Eggers, Dave. *This Bridge Will Not Be Gray*. San Francisco, CA: McSweeney's, 2015.

Hoena, Blake. *Building the Golden Gate Bridge: An Interactive Engineering Adventure*. North Mankato, MN: Capstone Press, 2015.

Online Story

Standen, Amy. "Life on The Gate: Working on the Golden Gate Bridge 1933–37." KQED Science website.

https://ww2.kqed.org/quest/2012/04/27/life-on-the-gate-working-on-the-golden-gate-bridge-1933-37

Video

HD Stock Footage Golden Gate Bridge Construction San Francisco Reel 2

https://www.youtube.com/watch?v=QxO1KvB4W10

See how the Golden Gate cables were spun in this historic film.

Index

Page numbers in **boldface** are illustrations. Entries in **boldface** are glossary terms.

anchorage, 14–16, **15**
bedrock, 14–15, 22
cables, 11, 14–19, **15**, **17**
compact, 18
compression, 13, **15**
Crocker, Charles, 8, **8**
current, 5, 14
fault, 14
ferry, **4**, 7–8
Golden Gate Strait, **4**, **7**, 8, 15
Gold Rush, 6
landmark, 5, 25, 27
loads, 13–14, 17–18
rivet, 21
Roebling, John, 18–19
safety, 23–25, **23**
sheath, 18
Strauss, Joseph, 9, **9**, 13, 18, 21, 23–26
suspenders, **15**, 17–18
tension, 13, **15**, 16–17
trestle, 22
wires, **16**, 17–18

Index 31

About the Author

Alicia Z. Klepeis began her career at the National Geographic Society. She is the author of numerous children's books including *Trolls*, *Haunted Cemeteries Around The World*, and *A Time For Change*. Alicia has crossed the Golden Gate Bridge in a car but hopes to walk across it someday.